Bi Bi,
Blue Eyed Boy

Lachlan Werner is a comic ventriloquist/satirist and writer. Since 2010 he has shocked and amused UK audiences with his subversive creations (including the all American, Uncle Alfie, and the egocentric, psychic celebrity, Brew the Witch) as well as appearing as a stage actor.

He has presented and toured his own ventriloquial stage shows, including *Who's Pulling the Strings?* (2014), *Pay no attention to the man behind the curtain* (2015) and *Belly Talk (A Language of Love)* (2017, Brighton Fringe).

His other books are *Summer Shorts* and *The Book of Nothing Kings.* In this, his first full collection of poetry, he blends memoir and gonzo-journalism as well as research in ethics and evolutionary biology, to explore themes of sexuality and gender as a clown.

Bi Bi, Blue Eyed Boy

LACHLAN WERNER

Bi Bi,
Blue Eyed Boy

Poems about sexuality

by a young clown in love.

Lulu Books

First edition

Published in paperback in America
By Lulu books 2017

ISBN- 978-0-244-62193-3

Rights to text and illustrations belong to Lachlan Werner and Wubbagocko
Ltd. 2017

To someone, one day

Ethics, like natural selection, make existence possible. Aesthetics, like sexual selection, make life lovely and wonderful, fill it with new forms, and give it progress, and variety and change."

Oscar Wilde

CONTENTS

Chapter 5:

Preface

According to the widely disputed theories of the novelist and biologist, Robin Baker, the more profusely romantically attracted to or jealously possessive a man feels towards a female sexual partner, the higher the quality of sperm he produces during their sex. By this I mean to say that the male will ejaculate considerably more semen and notably more 'kamikaze' sperm cells. These are-within Baker's somewhat dubious theory of 'sperm competition'-cells which have evolved as a second form of sperm (alongside 'Egg-Getters'-whose purpose is pretty emphatic in their name). 'Kamikaze' sperm has the assignment of totally annihilating rival 'Egg-Getters'-those produced by another man-in order to prevent them reaching the ovum of a female and fertilising it. They may do this through copious, astonishing methods, such as curling up in mucus, blocking the competitor 'Egg-Getters', or emitting a poison.

Baker's theories seem to evince-though unconvincingly to many-that for intentions of procreation, a man's insecurity or more compelling affinity for a woman subconsciously induces this response. To put it plainly, though alas, he doesn't know it, he wants to be her sole baby daddy.

Now if you are, at present, dispiritedly pondering on just why I might open a supposed collection of promisingly nonconformist romantic verse with research rooted wholly in the study of heterosexual pair-bonding, I apologise candidly. However, I'm certain there will be several readers, fascinated by Mr Baker's theory, asking the same ineluctable question as I...

'But what about homosexual men? Do *they* subconsciously jizz more and make fighting sperms that I imagine battle a bit like Jedi Starfighters? Even though *they* consciously know that their sexual liaisons won't result in procreation?'

Well, you delectably curious reader, I'm sorry and embittered when I confess that science and I have both here failed you. Though, presumably, a gay man-handling the same hormonal effects, the same insecurity and necessity for dominance as a straight one-wouldn't be at all dissimilar in what is, after all, a subconscious bodily function, I cannot *accurately* shed any light here. Unfortunately, this is not because biologists are attempting but are, as of yet, stumped in how precisely to approach research in this area.

Instead, it is merely a question of too little care. Nobody does. Did you, reader-who-is-almost-certainly-far-less-inquisitive-than-I-gave-you-credit-for, truly wonder about homosexuality's place in the equation of sperm competition? Or was that purely a crafty segue in this introduction? Now we're asking the real questions!

The point is none of those white-coated brainiacs, like the contentious Mr Baker, are concerned enough to labour themselves. Or so it would appear to me. Don't take my word for it, I'm no expert.

And neither, for that matter, is Robin Baker, whose other unorthodox, controversial and often abominably unsupported ideas can be found in his 1996 volume, *Sperm Wars.* From his and other theories on human sexuality, it seems disconcertingly perceptible to me that it's often more painless for scientists (or most heterosexual figures of eminence) to adopt a facile, even disregarding view on homo, bi, pan, tri, demi and asexual nature (to list but a handful).

We've still got so far to go.

I am bisexual. I have unabashedly indentified as such for almost six months, following a brief, moderately serene period of self-revelation. Although, Sigmund Freud notoriously claimed that all humans are born bisexual, so perhaps there was never, in fact, anything to be so conspicuously revealed.

The embracing of this ostensibly new component of my being was rather effortless. It was as though I had latently understood long ago just how fluent sexuality itself is, and was already organically prepared for this unearthing. However, what happened conclusively to this embryonic chapter is where the real tribulation begins.

I faced another ordeal as I began attempting to comprehend the unwritten rules of modern sexuality. Such a vast amount goes unuttered but is so widely, customarily understood. For instance, if a straight woman who is in a heterosexual relationship passionately kisses a gay man, no act of infidelity or treachery has been performed. Don't ask me why, I'm no expert.

I am a clown. My job is, to put it sentimentally, one in the cheering-up business. On stage, I am perennially fortunate in being masked by either a persona I adopt myself or a puppet-who, it is widely-known, are licensed to say anything they please, with a forgivable allure that penetrates political-correctness. I voice my most pertinent observations and impressions whilst an audience laughs. And yet, here in print, I am putting myself out in the open a little and telling a tenderly earnest and unfunny story. However, I'm still donning my guise as clown, for it's as equally exposing and humbling to be received as the buffoon you truthfully are as it is sheltering to hide within.

But for pertinence in these pages there shall be no unerring warrantee or promise. I can offer you-my acquiescent reader-only my totally subjective view. A visionary's ambition for this collection would certainly be apprising a still gravely ignorant predominance of society, or even giving some scant solace to someone reading from a closet (or yet another unconsidered position of distress). But my foolish, cynical clown-whose farcical, subjective tale this is to tell-is no idealist. He knows there is far too interminably rich a wealth of undisclosed complications to the nature of human sexuality and gender to surmise that his poetic offering should bring such change.

I am in love. This story is a love story. I am a horrible romantic, and this story is romantic. But the world needs not another overindulgent song versing heartache and yearning (though we are perpetually, grievously, universally lacking in 'queer' romantic mainstream content) and thus this work may be received, instead, as a study and vignette of our queer societal history.

The 'Blue Eyed Boy' depicted in the subsequent account truly enamoured me, galvanising an entire exploit of pain and scepticism. He inspired this book, a story that's gay without the glitter. For this-clownishly-I will love him for a long time. Sadly, it will never work out; he's more an Egg-Getter and I'm rather the accidental Kamikaze type.

Chapter 1:

In which the Young Clown meets the Blue Eyed Boy, causing the unearthing and fierce manifestation of some jolting new desires.

Blue Eyed Boy

Musician's favour

Play and pluck me like a bass;
Don't offer any heartfelt embrace,
Just let me lick your entire face
And walk away with affected, shameless grace.

Strum me like a violin,
Don't offer something earnest with meaning,
Just tickle and whip me and make me grin,
That would be the thing to lift my chin.

Beat on me like a set of drums,
Don't wonder why I've been so glum,
Yank my hair-it's harmless fun,
Just see what you have undone.

Dyspraxia at first sight

Here's an upfront list of every place
I've fallen over at the upfront thought of your face

I tripped on a chair leg in the room you practice in
And toppled over cables on the stage
I lost my footing at the park and fell into a bin
If only these fallible legs of mine would learn to behave.

I've rolled into gutters and tumbled from curbs
And collapsed in broad daylight on the street
I slid down stairs-that left me especially unnerved-
Oh, don't look so triumphant while you knock me off my feet.

Perhaps, it could be, the reason why
Is no man has ever looked this waif-like lad that way in the eye;
And though I be waggish, don't laugh, mister, when
I say I'd fall for you again and again.

Blue

Shall I take notice? 'READ THE LONG FORSAKEN NOTE'?
Struggle to pry open gifts for what the bag provokes?
For there's charm where it is crumpled, discoloured and turned dry
In the wrinkles 'neath those peaceful eyes, where smiles go to die.

The very shape of it-flexed arms and round derriere,
A smile so gently candid under lax greying hair-
Can cause a boy to flounder, negligent of himself.
Whose despotic design is this, causing abandonment to health?

It's the tempestuous key, that's burst my Pandora's box,
The carnivorous heart can't help devouring the ox.
It is the sole blue flag, out waving somewhere unseen and sad.
Holding unanswered wishes and ungiven gifts, it's a brown paper bag.

Touching that hand might turn me to dust,
But make scintillating glitter of what was plain crust.
The eyes are lit but sunken and tired;
I'll go to work straight 'way with the kind of tools required.

It might've been the maladroit manner you spun the straw to gold,
It might just be a sloppy tale of heart-ache that's ages old.
It might be merely nature-a thousand times had to be brave,
It might be it's been twenty years and he's too deep in to save.

You made yourself a paper bag from scraps you somehow found,
And tightly withhold the recherché gifts you know are there inside.
But each day I'm tearing holes, tenebrous bits of paper flutter around,
Iridescent blue eyed joy is leaking, and you've no-where left to hide.

Shock confession

Don't mind.
They don't.
Everyone knew before you.

I&U

I listen to old songs, about lovers
'So Rare'
And those you get sentimental
about.
My thoughts turn to you now, the
life we might live;
How one day, we'll share a house.

I imagine wandering out into the sea
On a weekend away for two —
I think of your hands, walking around
my body.
And I think that's the only
life that will do.

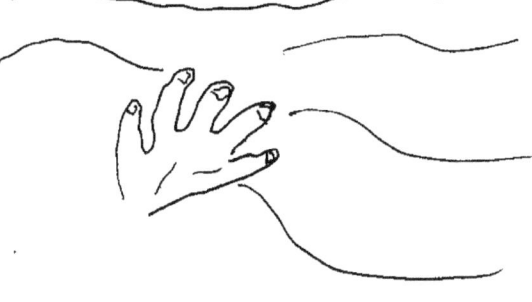

*Young Clowns are, inherently, horrible flirts.

Chapter 2:

In which the Young Clown discovers the Blue Eyed Boy's heterosexual affections for a girl (whom we will call 'His Girlfriend'-for that is what she is), encounters a poisoned, delirious young man and faces the unfamiliar stumble of a gender identity crisis.

Blue Eyed Boy

Sting

Where's that excruciating little thing
That every new love brings?
Ah–there it is.

Did I think you'd be another reason
I'd be so lost for another season?
Ah–of course.

Did I think that you'd hospitably let me in,
To only bring around that familiar sting?
Ah–I should've.

OUCH.

Sleeping with her

Witless gentle man, don't let her lie so close.
Though if you must, by obligation-since it was she that you chose-
Let her not see your mellow face; turn it disdainfully away!
And silently protest her lust, in the knowing that you're *quite*gay.

There's a young man waiting solitudinously, thirsty to be in her place
For he knows tonight, though she be close, there shan't be an unfeigned embrace.
You'll humour her with tales of fruitless life in her absence,
And not let on all week you've gleaned your joy in hot morsels and fragments.

Is he such an ignominious secret; that patient, neurotic young man?
You know he is the one whose hand falls impeccably into your hand.
But on this discomposed eve, beside her galling head you'll lay down-
Her head aloft in tedium-a queen unworthy of her crown.

If you happen to dine out with both-*if*circumstances are such-
Then lean upon that angular young man, I'm certain he'll be your crutch.
Survey him all the evening long, and note how he mirthfully lingers.
And don't wince, oh witless gentle man, when below the table you interlock fingers.

Be true to her, for *he*won't settle or rest contentedly you know;
But draw gratification from the spirit he affords before he goes!
He is your sordid confidante-or side bitch-there to be ignored.
Perhaps you'd ought to kiss him sharp, he won't wait longer to be anything more.

This night though, indulge the girl who travelled countless miles to see you,
And about the young man on your mobile phone tell her you frankly have no clue.
Tell her you've not the faintest notion why that boy won't go away;
And though tonight she'll see you're *quite*dry, tell her you're *quite*sure you're not gay.

Ketamine Ignoramus

He traipses, unassumingly, in after a night on Ketamine
With his old public school friends in a field.
He senses no disquiet or tension, and has no cause for intervention,
When the kamikaze words he hurls make no-one reel.

He invades a conversation, about homos and our creation,
And says 'But it can't be natural, it's just choice.
It's ageless, there in black and white; it's man and wife like day and night;
And you can't make babies bumming other boys.'

And not a soul utters a thing to the mop haired bigot on Ketamine
In his tie dye shirt and loose faded jeans.
For why commit an act of treason to this mere foolish king of unreason?
It's heedless but serene, to simply not ask what he means.

'If you're born with a cock, male is your gender–don't question me on this one, bender–
And giving your dong a good tuck doesn't make you a queen.
There aren't forty fucking orientations, just two clear persuasions
Either you're a real man who likes a nice bird, or you're into the peen.'

'A man *might* dig another man, but what in Shaggy's name is Pan?
And there's no such thing as Bi or Tri, this modern bullshit is a lie.
And who the fuck are you, you little prick, to say I'm wrong on all this shit,
While you're the one pitifully trailing after some straight guy?'

Question

Would not these messages still be the same
If I were not male or you were gay?

Womanhood

I would that I were female, with those advantageous wobbly bits–
Do tell me I'm hysterical; beseech me to get a grip–
But were I to wake one unclouded morn, without my dangling member,
Perhaps I'd have a whiter Christmas in gay Paree next December.

Were I enviable with red hair down to my waist–
The sort of elite demoiselle to meet your irrefutable taste–
Had I tanned, toned legs and teasing eyes to woo thee,
Perhaps I wouldn't be flying alone to gay Paree.

If my bustle were fleshier, or if you were a little less picky;
This might've all been somehow less exactingly tricky.
Don't miss my meaning, I *am* contented being a man,
But, this way, who will keep me warm in that remote, romantic land?

But, like woman, had I been endowed with 25% body fat,
Goodness knows a waif-like lad like I wouldn't be concerned with that!
I'd singlehandedly keep myself from freezing in bed with a fright,
While you'd be out playing in a jazz club in the misty Parisian night.

Since it is the unsightly appendage between my legs that repulses you,
Like the little mermaid who sliced out her tongue, I know what I must do.
Though I don't truly wish to be a woman, with all woman's labours and strife,
At least next winter in gay Paree, I know you'd make my Christmas white.

Chapter 3:

In which the Young Clown spends a long, confounding week with the Blue Eyed Boy and his comrades, and takes a remarkable and wild night out.

Hello! Want to come out with my friends and I tonight?

•Blue Eyed Boy•

Hey XD Sorry, got loads to do. But if you want a lift again this week let me know ;)

Uh... Alright... yeah I'll let you know...

x

Playfellows

Sitting, bemusedly, in the Kidderminster coffee shops,
With the beautiful girls, who dance blithely in the rain drops;
My Playfellows.

They chastise me, apprising me how I'm far 'too good for you'
And I yearn to believe it true;
They're the ones I ought to hearken to;
These Playfellows.

Every woman and Clown with a life debased by love knows
That doting Playfellows only turn to foes
While it cannot feasibly be true that I'll find 'better' than you;
Those deceitful Playfellows.

I spy them periodically, sitting with you,
And I am anguished, lest they too see into your eyes of blue,
And fall the same as I;
My risible Playfellows.

They see the coquetry in your smile,
And declare your magnetism for a modest while,
The charms they tally, I've doted on, for what seems like centuries gone;
What inattentive Playfellows.

And they detest my tedious sinking,
The beautiful, penetrating women;
Desirable Playfellows.

Who propose that *companionship must be foremost,* and postulate that *I'm 'better' than you*
Then take the Young Clown out, and desert him for the men they find there, as if on cue;
Such outlandish Playfellows.

In his car

I'm a beg, but when I implored you give me a ride home
And cocked my head
And pouted as amorously as I could,
I think, in sincerity,
I anticipated and hoped for
Your decline.

You acceded my demand.
'You know you love me,' I mocked.

> *'I know I love you,'* you giggled and flushed, and misplaced your balance.
> What?
> Daffodils grow in my skull.

'No, you don't really have to. You live forty minutes from me.'

> *'I don't mind. Just a one off.'*
> I succumb-growing toward the light you lend from every direction, and roses
> Bloom on the soles of my feet, treading me
> With boundless edge
> To a yellow car.

> *'Just climb in there. Do you mind holding my bass?'*
> Buds on my fingertips, I grasp the instrument. Take it
> Between my thighs as
> A partner.
> As a seed I am planting. This piece
> Of *you.*

I want to grow. Envelop every inch of this yellow car
In my vegetation.
Stifle and swallow it.
My roots plunge deeper into the foundation.
Soil. *You.*

I feel ease.

You.

We look like a pair.

'How are you?' I pray *'You look tired.'*

You give a doleful nod. Dahlias trail and stretch

Beneath us on a night-time motorway.

> *'I am. My girlfriend is going out tonight with some friends.*
>
> *It's fine.'*
>
> There's her.
>
> I'm unkempt.
>
> The garden you cannot
>
> Maintain.

I'm eager to climb the trellis, the wall.

Let my ivory spill into your garden.

Filling your car.

My baggage. *You.* Your backseat.

My flowers in your garden.

Don't you see

My undergrowth

Thriving

Burgeoning

Through your glove compartment? Your radio?

> *'Whereabouts is it?'*

'Just here.'

> *'The park?'*

'This will do.'

You shan't drive to my house

What would the neighbours say if

They saw

The car shaped flower-bed out on the street?

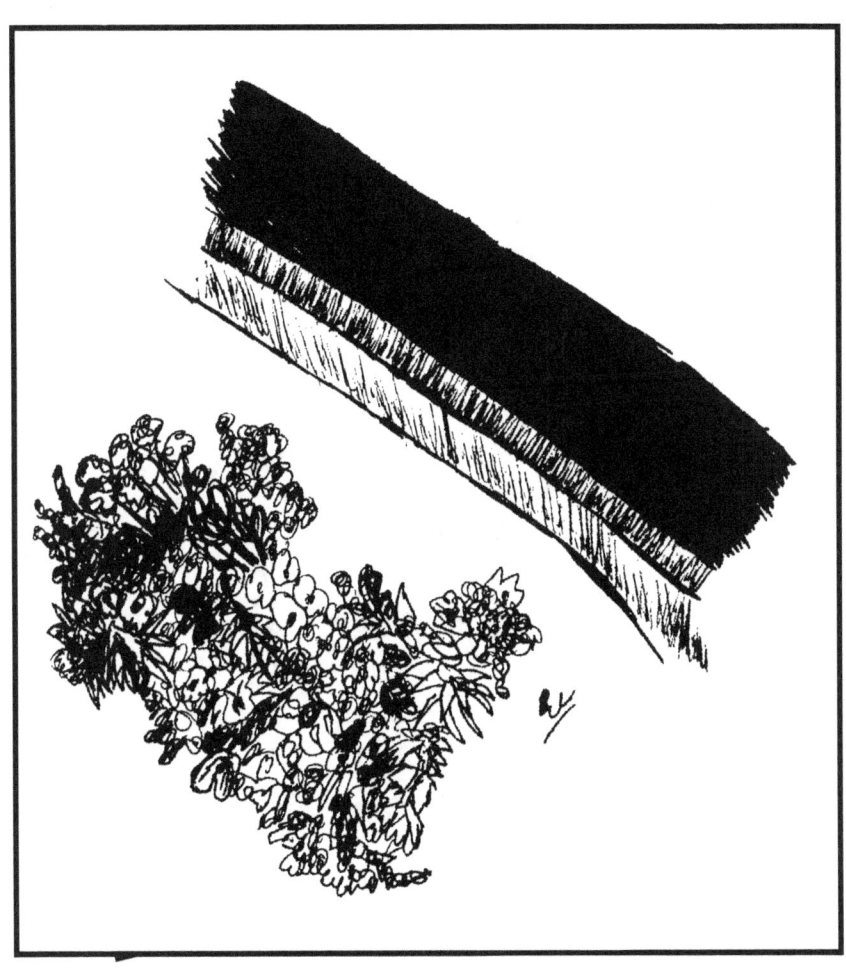

Onus

This is not MUTUAL APPREHENSION

This is YOUR COWARDICE

Dancing tongue

While out and rather wine-drenched, in a licentious club called Sin
How was a waif-like lad to know the melting-pot of libidos he was in?
And when you teetered over on towering heels, how did you know
That I was bi, and to a naughty, lascivious try, I wouldn't say no?

While we were playfellows and blathering, where was my impeachable foresight?
You were bent on sampling goods before we danced away that decadent night.
And you were the most arresting babe my drifting, spellbound eyes could note
So when you tugged me down upon that love-seat, how could I say no?

While the 'banging tunes' thundered and acrylic nails brushed my back
I must've known your silken body was a cajoling, winding track.
Dirty blonde hair fugaciously kissed my face, arousing me so.
And with your roaming tongue inside my mouth, I couldn't say no.

I want a dancing tongue like yours, that glissades and ventures.
So unfettered did it slide-so euphorically-that you must've forgotten to mention
That dallying nearby was your boyfriend, and less than blithe was he;
Yet, though he caught you in my caress, you said he had no cause to be.

While we blundered to our feet, apologising gravely,
You, unscrupulous seductress, you conjured a sharp defence readily.
For when you said, 'listen babe-he's gay, if you must know,'
And asked if he was vexed still, how could *he* say no?

Blonde twink disposable

He was a young man sitting solitudinously-
This much remains perspicuous in my memory-
He was clad in stripes and pert, tight black dungarees;
I seized him by the hand and urged him, 'dance with me?'

But they weren't those worn, benign pink fingers.

As he enounced my charms into my ear,
I detected the moderate stroke of a thin beard,
And since I was inspired, I heaved him near;
My tongue danced a tango and he was forced to yield.

But it wasn't his mouth I imagined I was kissing.

Fetish

That girl in the black dress, wiv the longish brown hair;
Look closah, babes, I can see her underwear.
The fishnet stockings propah give it away-
Go for it, babes, I reckon she's gay.

Get in and ask her for a cheeky little snog,
Do it ovah here, just ou'side the bogs.
Yeah I swear, I'll make sure all the fellas'll watch it,
She's pretty much plastahed, just don't flippin' well botch it!

Make her inky black lipstick smear,
And it's those sticky little sounds we'll want ta hear.
It's just one time, babe, give it a whirl,
You know the boys love a bit a' 'girl on girl'.

Oh God, 'ave a look, she's nodded off-ah shit.
Nah don't worry, babe, you can still do it!
I'm sure she won't mind, sweets, it's what she's into;
Get on wiv it, girl, that lad wiv the hair'll be all ovah you!

I know, babe, it's a bit risky, this game you're playin';
What if she reckons all night you'll be stayin'?
Just say 'sorry babe' and tell her the same fing I always do:
'Only when I'm on the piss am I in-ta dykes like you.'

Question II
(on the curb)

Would I be here-so lost and perturbed-
Shivering feebly out here on a curb?
If you were here and dancing with me tonight,
Would not you just hold me and make me alright?

Mate, that song I wrote is shit. XD

Haha don't worry, while I'm gone, my girlfriend can make me cry myself to sleep ;)

I'm not bi...

Chapter 4:

In which the Young Clown learns to distract himself with the study of his human sexuality and his new intrigue of his queer friends.

Blue Eyed Boy

The blessing

Hitting the spot

With the plastic wand,
The plunger,
The broom handle,
The shampoo bottle,
And the hairbrush
All with that unequivocal touch
Lacking,

I am not
Precisely
What some might call
'Cracking'.

Boyfriend under my bed

I bought myself a boyfriend,
And stashed him inconspicuously under my bed.
And if my mother happens to find him there
My face will turn a coruscating red.

I bought him at a local *Boots*
For nineteen pounds, ninety nine.
Though at first I feared he'd be simply too big
It so happens he's just fine.

And so I squeeze in

Time for him,
Whilst I am unescorted
And as I do, loitering in my mind,
Are foolish things you have retorted.

But you'd be a redundant boyfriend;
I cannot stow *you* beneath my bed.
And if my mother discovered *you*
My face would turn an effulgent red!

Potpourri Ignoramus

by Brew the Witch

I'm sure his mother always was a bit *worried* about him
Lest he might turn out that way.
It wasn't as if no~one had an eerie old inkling
That little Lachy might've been *a gay...*

Well Poppets, I don't care one iota~
Look, it makes no odds to me~
And I'm sure his family are just as warmly welcoming~
They were a tad surprised he still liked girls, you see /

But he wouldn't say *boo to a goose*, that boy,
He won't be going to Pride or any of that malarkey.
I don't see much pertinent point in it myself~
They've got their rights now~no need to be *OTT!*

There was a couple of them who used to live next~door~but~one,
They caused no fuss~they were a *real* delight /
Although, every once in a blue moon you *would* hear them...
Doing God knows what, on a Friday night...

Please, Darls', don't think I'm saying it's dreadfully distasteful~
I don't want the poor ducks to stay hushed /
I'm sure we've *all* had such a funny old phase~
In school I even once had a girl crush /

And don't fret, Loveys, no don't panic~
Whether he gets past this tense little trouble or not.
He's still the same stupe Sweetheart
And we'll love him no matter what.

XoXo

Delivered

Observe the healed man, God has saved;
Don't question the glassy stare of trepidation so grave.
Espy the Oxford blue suit and mustard yellow bow-tie
Hear the Gospel Jazz reverb, and worship something up in the sky.

'I would NOT date a man. I would NOT bear a purse,'
He squalls and spasms, liberated of a nocuous curse.
'I AM delivered! I don't like MENS NO MORE!'-
A doubtful gift from a magnanimous Lord.

'I will LOVE A WOMEN, WOMEN!' He gibbers and so
To some celestial place the contused man shall go.
It was worth the harrowing cost, betrayed by the paler hues of his face,
His miracle transmutation means an awaiting, divine embrace.

Demisexuality

We think it so alien now
That someone should want
Their soul touched
Before
Anything else

That there is
A necessity
For a label.

A Pantasmagoric romance

Perhaps 'tis we who spread the disease,
Perhaps we're the ravenous flea-bags.
Perhaps we're desperate, craving and voracious
Or perhaps they're disaffected old drags.

Perhaps it's true, it's degenerate and unintended by nature,
Perhaps we're unfit to confer full attention.
Perhaps we're unwittingly inclined to disloyalty
Or perhaps their hypothesising is total pretension.

Perhaps 'tis we who are wanton and indecent;
The gender-blind jezebels who grasp and smack and shove.
Perhaps we cleave to an evolutionary perk,
Or perhaps they merely can't comprehend plain love?

We're transfiguring the [...]
not merely because we be but blithe
But because history's unenlight[...]
Shan't be Obeyed
Down with the chaste, white frills [...]
being 'given away!'

of our uniting lovers, both bodies are
possessors of their own,
without expectations of a gender-role
inside a tarnished home.
So without the shadows of slavery
Bedevilling hetero-wedded life
Down with pronouncing heaven-made matches
'man and wife'.

Two-thousand-and-fourteen

We're transfiguring the 'happy day',
Not merely because we be but blithesome gays
But because history's unenlightened lunacy shan't be obeyed-
Down with the chaste, white-frilled virgin being 'given away'.

Of our uniting lovers, both bodies are possessors of their own,
Without expectations of a gender-role inside a typical tarnished home.
So without shadows of the slavery, bedevilling hetero-wedded life
Down with pronouncing heaven-made matches, 'man and wife'.

Chapter 5:

In which the Young Clown tires of the Blue Eyed Boy at last, leaving him behind for an auspiciously romantic future, while all that remains is his perpetual gratitude for the queer exploits to come... all because of his love of music!

•Blue Eyed Boy•

Ganymede

If you were Ganymede-strapping and ebullient-
And I, the shape-shifting winged Zeus,
I believe, somewhere in my flight-
In the pursuit of the object of all my lust-
I've dropped you.

Question III
(on platform 2)

I think no future can ever harm
The memory of that moment, so full of charm,
When sitting solitudinously on platform two
I gazed up across the way to spy no-one but you.

Will you remember me, and the moment we smiled?
The way we simpered at each other for a little while?
Will you read this book and sit thinking 'Well hey,
Imagine writing all of this, even after I boarded that train.'

Haircut

That long, rakish dark hair-like the locks of Oscar Wilde-
Was somehow the esoteric key to the way you had beguiled.
I've put our scandal to trial; call me Douglas, here's your arrest-
You're no aesthete or sodomite, but you put my spine to the test.

What knavish trickery- slicking back your greying strands!
And foolish I, trusting you'd hacked it away, with such breezy hand.
Such an ethereal face-so reoriented-so foreign to my eye-
I begged of you to never change; thank heavens this turn was a lie.

'That isn't love you know,' proclaims the waif-like lad to himself
'Love is falling again through swivelling seasons, through sickness and health'
So do I love this man whose thrall I've been under in this state of obfuscation?
Can my love be so plastic? Can a haircut be such a fracturing alteration?

But your unruly mane's your essence-like the dapper Wilde, you're a petit-maître.
And does not my rash relief betray an affinity for a lifeblood beyond hair?
Or else, alas, I love purely the blue eyed outer-shell of you-it's true.
But you're pleading guilty; so call me Douglas, for I still love our type of taboo.

She&U

I think of the two of you, wandering
    on our weekend beach —
Never wetting your feet.
The dream of your hand, walking around
    my body
Is tossed into the surf
    and drifts out of reach.

I imagine your future; your work and
        your sex
And how you might wear your hair
My thoughts turn to me — the beauties
        I'll behold —
A life without you, and I don't think
        I care.

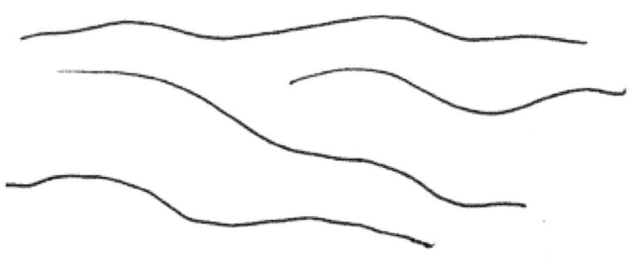

Bi Bi

We once sat in your yellow car and listened to Bowie
Now we're here in a licentious club called Sin, and dancing blithely.
And over totters another Clown and another Blue Eyed Boy-
One waif-like lad who'll never betray all that his playfellow does exploit.

And this time your tired blue eyes seem to spy
That gleam of a fool's adulation so shy.

They dance and you muse that his friend, so blind,
Has never even pondered l'amour of that kind
And I tell you, in total earnest, that it will be fine-
The Clown will survive and thrive, and smile, in time.

And though, of course, from you I yearned for so much more
Now I see all I have to thank you for.

Despite all the holes I attempted to tear,
I know it's not much like you to really dare.
But thank you for sending me to gay Paree alone;
Think of the room my flowers shall have to grow.

Think of my outlandish Playfellows, who were perpetually right,
For I don't require you here holding me tonight.
But thank you for granting my heart that familiar sting
You reminded me of all the love inside that bruised old thing.

Think of the ignoramuses I'll prove to be mistaken
Think of all the intoxicating trials I have undertaken.
But thank you for rousing all these melancholy questions for you
For in a forage for answers I've absorbed so much too.

Think of the tribulations I'm yet to see
And the beguiling brown paper bagged prizes that will never come free.
But thank you for the fantasies of our beach and the nights I cried;
Your yellow car was ideal practice for an imminent bumpy ride.

And stay true to her, for I won't settle or rest contentedly, you know-
I hope you've drawn gratification from all I afforded, now it's time to go.
I'm taking down the sole blue flag to leave way for a rainbow one,
Although I never got to see if, truly, you know how have fun.

But it meant a lot at the time, mister-even if it was cruel-
When the blue eyed musician told me I was cool.

Afterword and organisations

Thank you, reader, for staying so attentively with me until here. However I have just a brief few thoughts and sources of progress left to leave you with.

First I'd like to urge you to remember this: despite what Kate Nash says, we must all give a fuck about the agendas of one another. We can change absolutely nothing without compromise and conversation, and we give ourselves no right to be heard when we refuse to listen. Ignoramuses are often insufferable, I grant you this, but first hear them out before advocating them with your ideas and view of the world.

Secondly, if you are a hetero reader I extend an especially gracious thanks and congratulations to you. Empathy is something the world is, at last, learning the potency of and you are a contributor to this! I ask you merely to hold on to this vigorously, and continue to question daily your views, and tirelessly research the subjective struggles of individuals everywhere–there is an eternal wealth of remarkable stories to be told. And, more than anything remain as unbiased and neutral as you possibly can when it comes to your own sexual experiments and endeavours. Permit yourself the space to unearth exciting aspects of yourself.

The following list of both charitable organisations and research materials is not exhaustive but provides a variety of online areas and printed work aimed at addressing some issues raised in this book, as well as giving reference to some of the better sources of learning I've found:

CHARITIES:

http://www.stonewall.org.uk/ (A charity dedicated to helping let LGBTQ+ people know they're not alone.)

http://www.hrc.org/ (Human Rights Campaign)

http://www.ifge.org/ (International Foundation for Gender Education)

https://lnfy.org/ (Lost-N-Found Youth organisation, whose aim is to give more permanent housing to homeless LGBTQ+ young people) https://www.brook.org.uk/ (Charity working to provide better sex and relationships education in schools and to young people online)

READING:

Sperm Wars by Robin Baker

Bisexuality and Queer Theory edited by Jonathon Alexander and Serena Anderlini-D'Onofrio

A Concentric Theory of Human Sexuality by Daniel Poole (I have decided to make an example of this one as the type of pitifully under-researched work that misinforms thousands of people-this book inspired the poem 'A Pantasmagoric romance')

Queering Religion, Religious Queers edited by Yvette Taylor and Ria Snowdon

Animal. The Autobiography of a Female Body by Sara Pascoe

An Anthology Of Erotic Verse edited by Derek Parker (almost devoid of queer content but not quite)

A Queer Little History of Art by Alex Pilcher

The Unmasking of Oscar Wilde by Joseph Pearce (for wonderful insight on my personal favourite gay literary figure).

Acknowledgements

I would to thank the following people for bringing this book to a surprise fruition: Richard Hyman for the name, the editing and assistance team at Lulu books for permitting the publication of my first queer volume, Sin and Bushwackers, Worcester and Brighton Fringe Festival for direct access to locations to Gonzo journalism.

Chloe Wilson: for proof-reading, offering guidance to countless sources of research and inspiration, for hundreds of the finest, most stimulating conversations about the nature of love and, most of all, for a friendship so intense and loving I can no longer envisage life without it. If I believed in soulmates, I'd be certain you were mine.

My best friends, Rachael Dodd, Humaira Khan, Millicent Haywood, Sophie Rutherford, Connor Mcgee and Poppy Janisch for all the support on this project and others. I'd also like to give special thanks to Scarlett Richards for innumerable titbits of advice and for sharing inspiring opinions from the offset of the 'blue eyed' struggle.

To my siblings, Mali and Islan, for giving me all the conceivable room to express everything I've ever cared to, and for constantly inspiring me and making me smile. To my father, for taking my most irrational behaviour and bursts of self-frustration with a 'pinch of salt'.

My mother, for accepting all I have evolved to-in its ugliness, despair, idiocy and pleasure-for supporting me (morally, emotionally and financially) through all, for handling the tears of a heartbreak and the incessancy of a rude activist. For loving and dedicating a life to the queer ventriloquist clown.

Finally, to the blue eyed boy: there's nothing else to be said but thank you for the adventures to come, for holding a mirror to me and making me cry and feel monstrous and spiky and untouchable and, sometimes, beautiful. Thank you for the confusion, life of late might've been so plain otherwise.